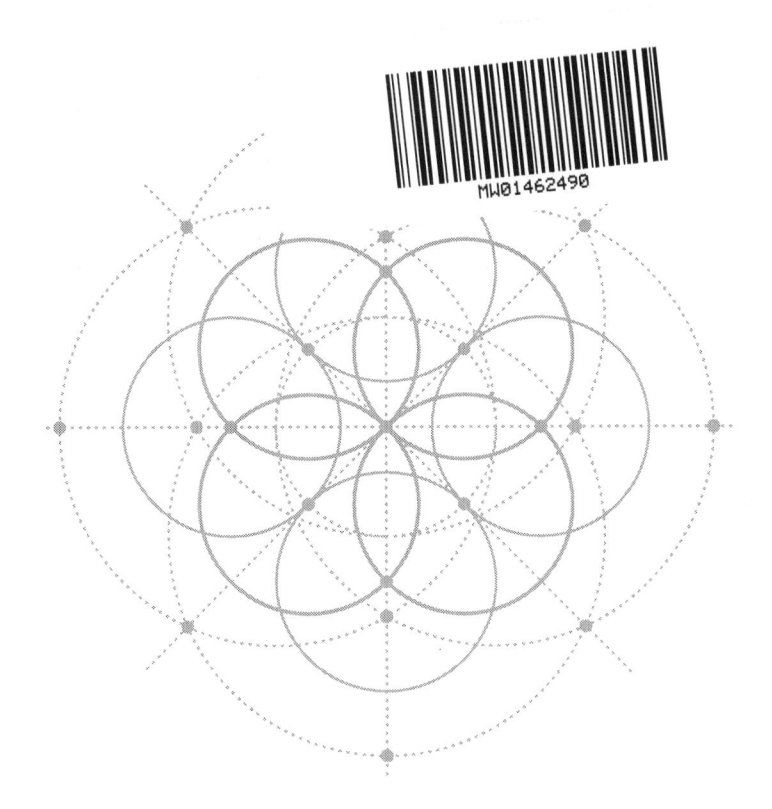

A Thought Journal
for
Human Design
Manifestors

Human Design

The Human Design System is a holistic personality and life mapping tool that combines various esoteric and scientific disciplines, including astrology, the I Ching, the Kabbalah, and quantum physics. It was 'downloaded' by Robert Allan Krakower, thereafter known as Ra Uru Hu, during meditation in 1987 and has since gained popularity as a unique system for understanding human behaviour, decision-making, and life purpose.

At its core, Human Design proposes that each individual is born with a specific energetic blueprint, known as a BodyGraph or a Human Design Chart. This chart is calculated using the individual's birth data, including the date, time, and place of birth. The chart provides a visual representation of the individual's energetic centres, channels, and gates. Since you're here, it's likely that you already know some of the details of your Human Design. You can find the basic elements of your chart for free on many different websites, and if you would like an individual reading there are likewise many readers available to consider. I would be happy to do a reading for you, and you can find my details on my website at www.grasshopperandbee.com.

Human Design recognises five main types of individuals: Manifestor, Projector, Generator, Manifesting Generator, and Reflector. Each type has its unique strategy and way of engaging with the world. These types are determined by the openness or definition of certain energetic centres in the chart.

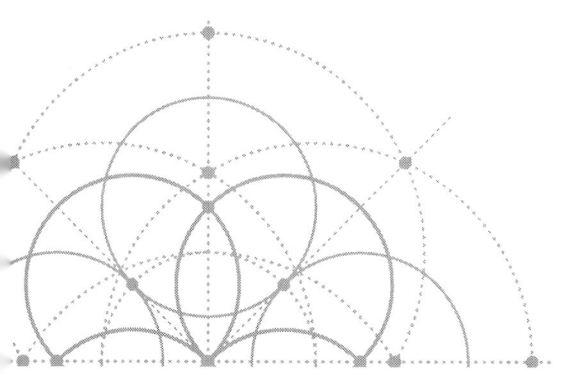

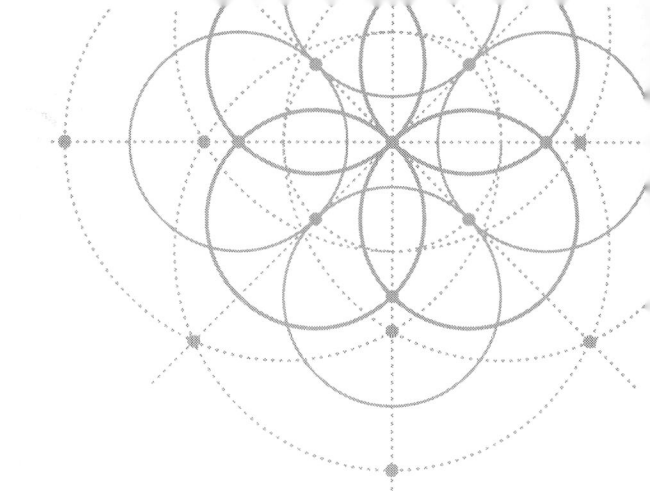

The system also encompasses other components such as authority, centres, channels, gates, and profiles, which provide further insights into an individual's decision-making process, energy dynamics, and life experiences. The information in a Human Design chart can be used to understand one's strengths, challenges, life purpose, and how to navigate decision-making in alignment with their true nature.

Human Design encourages people to live according to their inner authority, which refers to the decision-making process that is most authentic for them. Each type and authority has a different way of making decisions, such as listening to their gut response, waiting for clarity, or discussing with others. By honouring your unique decision-making process, you can align with your natural flow and make choices that lead you to a more fulfilling and authentic life.

It's important to note that Human Design is not a predictive system and does not determine one's future. Instead, it offers a map of your energetic makeup and suggests ways to navigate life in alignment with your true nature. The system is designed to empower you to live your life authentically, make decisions that are in harmony with your design, and cultivate self-awareness and self-acceptance.

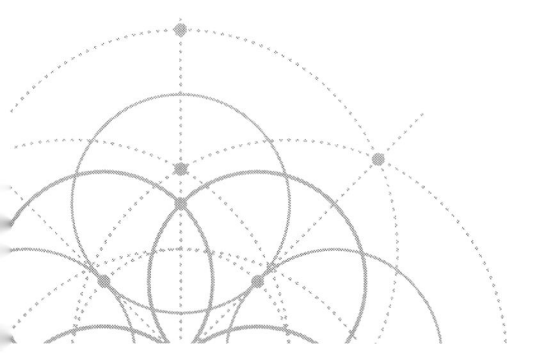

Manifestors

In the Human Design system, a Manifestor is one of the five main types of individuals. Being a Manifestor means you have a specific energetic aura and a unique way of engaging with the world. Manifestors are approximately 9% of the population. Here are some key aspects of being a Manifestor:

Energetic Aura

As a Manifestor, you have a closed and repelling aura. This means your energy is self-contained and can impact the energy of others around you. I prefer to think of it as protective, allowing you to create and initiate without energetic influence from others. Your aura is designed to initiate and get things started, but it can also create a sense of resistance in others.

Initiators

Manifestors have a natural ability to initiate actions and bring about change. You are often driven by a strong sense of inner knowing and a need to make things happen. Your purpose is to bring your unique visions and ideas into reality.

Autonomy and Independence

Manifestors thrive when they have the freedom to act independently and follow their own impulses. You have an innate need for autonomy and may find it challenging to follow rules or be controlled by others.

Impact on Others

Your energy can be intense and influential, and it's important to be aware of how it affects those around you. Informing others about your plans and actions can help prevent resistance and allow for smoother interactions.

Rest and Recharge

Manifestors have a cyclical energy pattern and may experience bursts of energy followed by periods of rest. It's crucial for you to honour your need for downtime and rejuvenation to maintain balance and well-being.

Strategy

The Manifestor type has a unique strategy called "Inform Before Acting." It involves informing those who may be impacted by your actions before taking any major steps. This strategy helps build trust and minimises resistance from others.

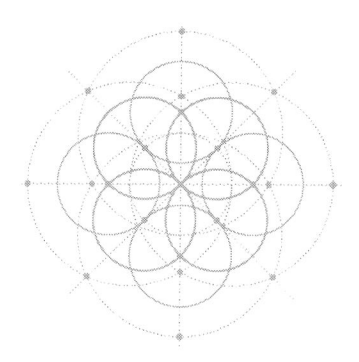

Remember, the Human Design system provides a framework to understand your energetic makeup, but it is just one perspective among many. Exploring your own experiences and finding what resonates with you is key to gaining a deeper understanding of yourself as a Manifestor.

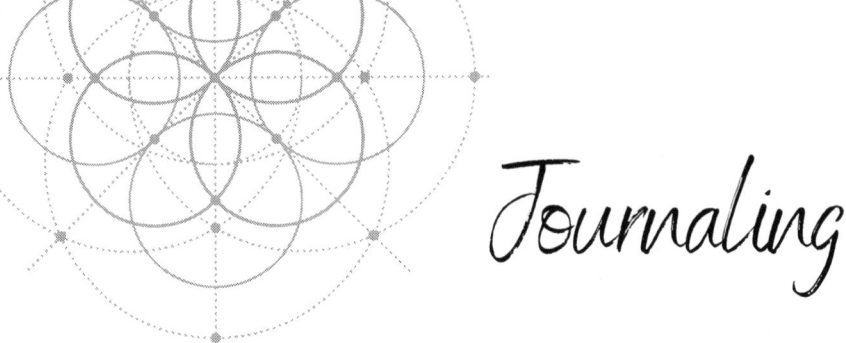

Journaling

Journaling is a powerful practice that offers numerous benefits for personal growth, self-reflection, and overall well-being. Here are a few advantages of incorporating journaling into your daily routine:

Self-Exploration and Reflection

Journaling provides a safe space for self-expression and exploration. By putting pen to paper, you can delve into your thoughts, feelings, and experiences. It allows you to gain insights into yourself, your values, and your aspirations. Journaling facilitates self-reflection, helping you process emotions, identify patterns, and gain clarity on your life's journey.

Emotional Release and Stress Reduction

Writing in a journal can be a therapeutic outlet for emotional release. It allows you to unload and process pent-up emotions, reducing their intensity and providing a sense of relief. Journaling can serve as a form of self-care, helping you manage stress, anxiety, and overwhelm. It offers a private space where you can freely express yourself without judgment.

Goal Setting and Manifestation

Journaling is a valuable tool for setting and manifesting goals. By writing down your aspirations, dreams, and action plans, you clarify your intentions and make them more tangible. Journaling helps you break down big goals into smaller steps, track your progress, and celebrate achievements along the way. It serves as a roadmap to keep you focused and motivated on your desired outcomes.

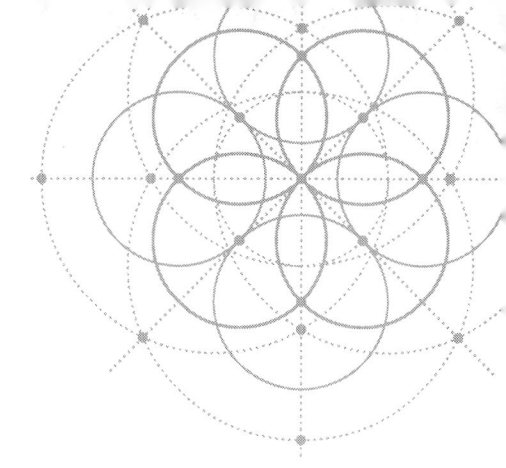

Enhanced Creativity and Problem-Solving

Writing in a journal stimulates your creative thinking and problem-solving abilities. It opens up channels for new ideas, insights, and perspectives. When you engage in free-flowing journaling, without worrying about grammar or structure, you tap into your subconscious mind and access fresh insights. Journaling can help you generate creative solutions, gain different perspectives on challenges, and cultivate a deeper understanding of yourself.

Self-Awareness and Personal Growth

Regular journaling fosters self-awareness and personal growth. It allows you to observe and analyse your thoughts, behaviours, and beliefs over time. By recognizing patterns and identifying areas for improvement, you can actively work towards personal development and positive change. Journaling helps you track your progress, celebrate milestones, and develop a stronger sense of self.

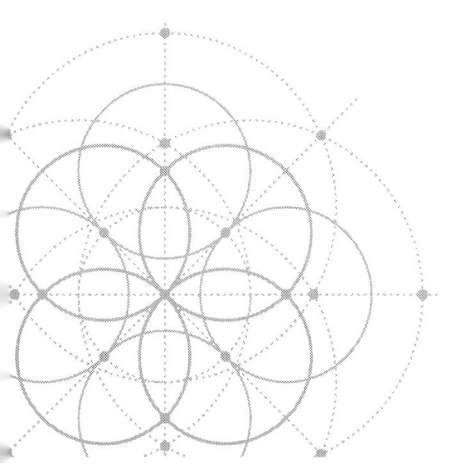

This Journal

Remember, there is no right or wrong way to journal. It's a personal practice, and you can customise it to suit your needs and preferences. Whether you choose to write stream-of-consciousness, gratitude lists, or structured prompts, the key is to make journaling a regular habit that supports your well-being and growth.

What follows in this book is a series of prompts designed to act as a jumping off point. If the answers to these questions or suggestions take you in entirely unexpected directions, that's totally fine. If it's easier for you to write your answers as bullet points, as spider diagrams, as letters to your younger self, as sketches, as an uninterrupted stream-of-consciousness, or in any other way that comes to you, then that is the right way. I repeat - there's no wrong way of doing this! However you journal is the right way for you. There are lined pages and blank pages; use them however you feel called to.

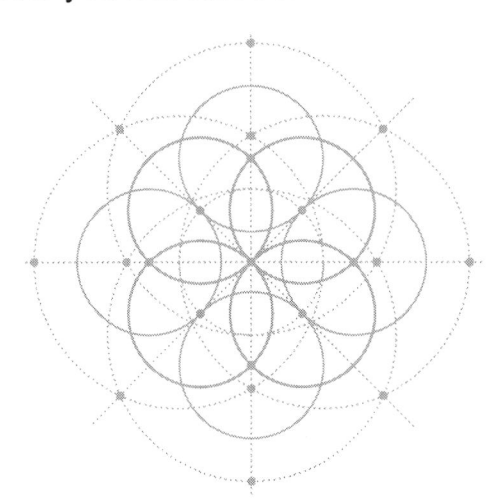

Gratitude

Gratitude is a powerful practice that can shift your perspective and cultivate a sense of abundance and appreciation. By focusing on gratitude specific to your Manifestor nature, you can deepen your understanding of yourself and embrace the unique gifts and opportunities that come with being a Manifestor in the Human Design system.

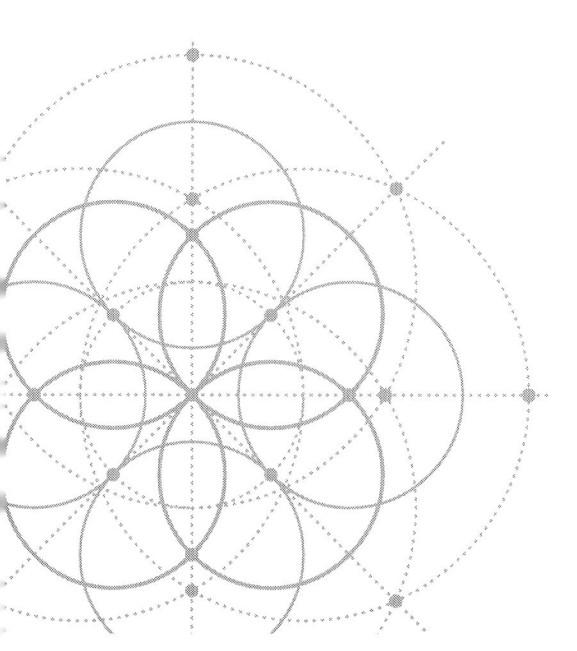

Gratitude for Initiating Change

Take a moment to reflect on the times when you initiated positive change in your life or in the lives of others. Consider the impact of your actions and the opportunities that arose from your ability to manifest and bring ideas into reality. Express gratitude for your innate power to initiate and create positive shifts. Even the smallest act of initiative counts - don't discount something just because it feels small. Sometimes the smallest changes can snowball into life-changing events, and sometimes small changes can signify a larger internal shift within you.

Gratitude for Autonomy and Independence

Consider the blessings and advantages of being an independent individual, no matter how big or small. Reflect on any freedom you have to follow your own impulses, make decisions without external validation, and carve your unique path. Express gratitude for the autonomy and independence that allows you to manifest your authentic self.

_____
_____
_____
_____
_____
_____
_____
_____
_____
_____
_____
_____
_____
_____
_____
_____
_____
_____
_____
_____
_____
_____

Gratitude for Supportive Relationships:

Reflect on the people in your life who have embraced and supported your Manifestor nature. Consider those individuals who have understood and honoured your need for autonomy and have been there to lend a helping hand or provide guidance when needed. Express gratitude for the relationships that have fostered your growth and empowered you to manifest your true potential.

_____
_____
_____
_____
_____
_____
_____
_____
_____
_____
_____
_____
_____
_____
_____
_____
_____
_____
_____
_____

Gratitude for Rest and Rejuvenation

Recognise the importance of rest and rejuvenation in your life as a Manifestor. Consider the moments when you have honoured your cyclical energy pattern and allowed yourself to recharge. Express gratitude for the times when you've listened to your body's need for rest, which has contributed to your overall well-being and vitality.

_____
_____
_____
_____
_____
_____
_____
_____
_____
_____
_____
_____
_____
_____
_____
_____
_____
_____
_____
_____
_____
_____
_____
_____
_____

Gratitude for the Power of Informing

Reflect on the times when you've successfully employed the strategy of informing before acting in your interactions with others. Consider how this approach has helped build trust, reduce resistance, and create harmonious connections. Express gratitude for the power of effective communication and the positive impact it has had on your relationships and collaborations.

Inner Child

Inner child work is a deeply personal and transformative process. These prompts are meant to guide you in exploring and healing the aspects of your inner child as a Manifestor. Approach the process with gentleness, compassion, and a willingness to reconnect with your true essence.

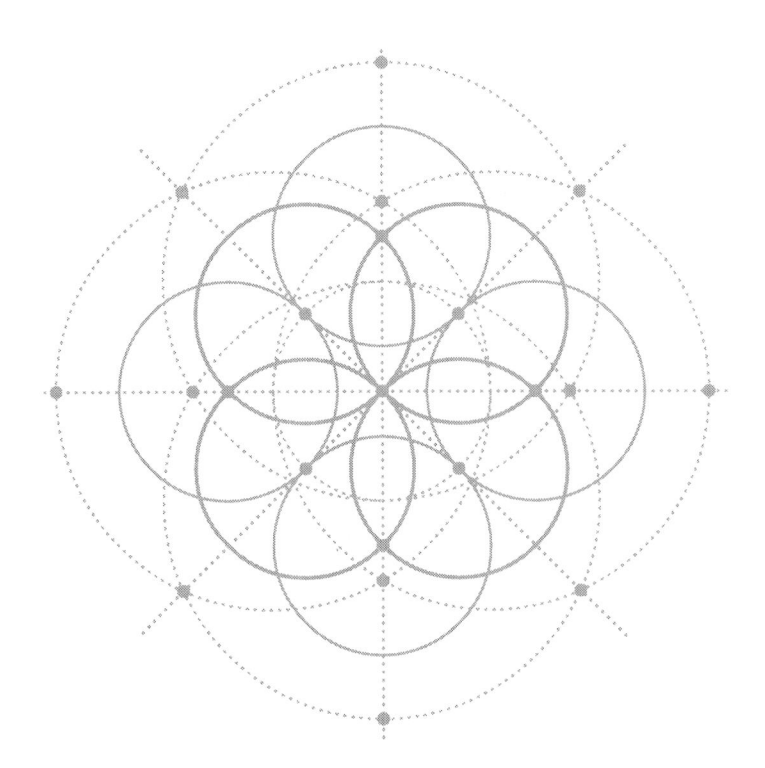

Nurturing Your Inner Child

Reflect on moments from your childhood when you felt the most free, joyful, and authentic. Consider activities, experiences, or qualities that brought out your true essence as a child. How can you nurture and integrate those aspects of your inner child into your adult life? Write about ways to reconnect with your inner child and bring more joy and playfulness into your present reality.

Honouring Autonomy and Independence

Explore how your inner child might have experienced a desire for autonomy and independence. Reflect on any instances where you felt restricted or controlled as a child. How can you provide support and understanding to your inner child's need for independence within healthy boundaries? Write about ways to honour your inner child's autonomy while maintaining harmony and balance in your life.

_____
_____
_____
_____
_____
_____
_____
_____
_____
_____
_____
_____
_____
_____
_____
_____
_____
_____
_____
_____
_____
_____
_____
_____
_____

Healing Past Wounds

Reflect on any past experiences or wounds from your childhood that may still affect you as an adult. Consider how these experiences might have influenced your Manifestor nature, such as fear of rejection or resistance to authority. How can you bring healing and compassion to these aspects of your inner child? Write about ways to release any lingering pain or limitations and embrace a sense of empowerment.

_____
_____
_____
_____
_____
_____
_____
_____
_____
_____
_____
_____
_____
_____
_____
_____
_____
_____
_____
_____
_____
_____
_____
_____

Embracing Spontaneity and Play

Tap into your inner child's natural sense of spontaneity, creativity, and playfulness. Reflect on activities or hobbies that used to bring you immense joy and explore how you can incorporate them into your present life. Write about ways to prioritise play and infuse a sense of lightheartedness into your daily routine as a means of reconnecting with your inner child's spirit.

_____
_____
_____
_____
_____
_____
_____
_____
_____
_____
_____
_____
_____
_____
_____
_____
_____
_____
_____
_____
_____
_____
_____
_____
_____
_____
_____

Reconnecting with Innocence and Trust

Explore your inner child's capacity for innocence, trust, and wonder. Reflect on any instances where your innocence might have been compromised or trust might have been broken. How can you rebuild a sense of trust and embrace the purity of your inner child's heart? Write about ways to foster a sense of trust, openness, and curiosity in your relationships and experiences as a Manifestor.

_____
_____
_____
_____
_____
_____
_____
_____
_____
_____
_____
_____
_____
_____
_____
_____
_____
_____
_____
_____
_____
_____
_____
_____
_____

Self-Kindness

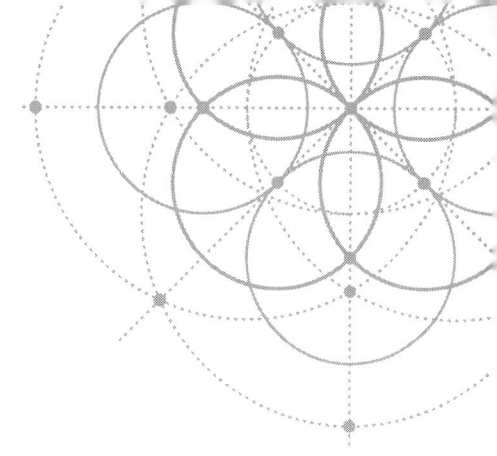

Self-kindness is an ongoing practice that requires patience and self-awareness. These prompts are intended to guide you in nurturing a compassionate relationship with yourself as a Manifestor. Approach the process with love, acceptance, and a commitment to honouring your own needs and experiences.

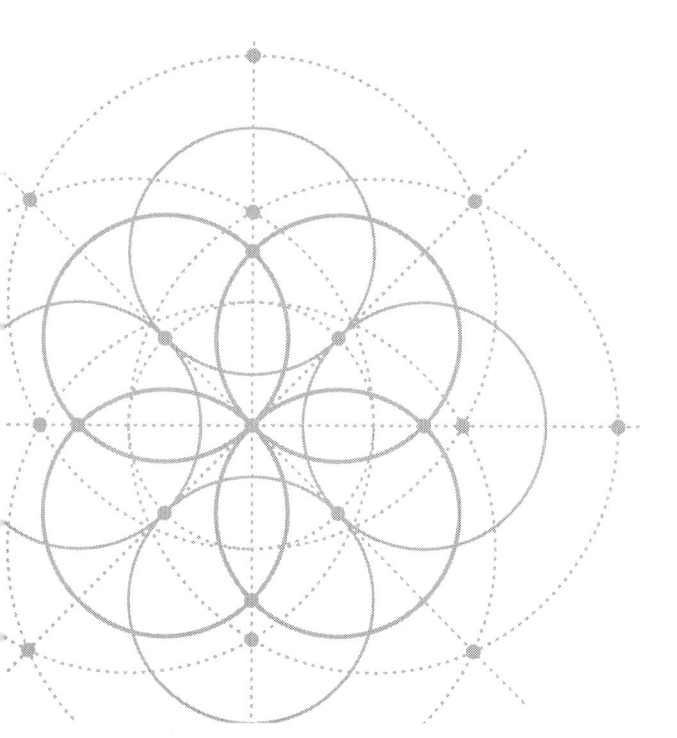

Embracing Your Unique Pace

Reflect on your natural energetic rhythm as a Manifestor. Consider the times when you may have felt pressured or judged for not conforming to societal expectations or timelines. How can you show yourself kindness by honouring your own pace and allowing yourself the time and space needed to initiate and manifest in alignment with your authentic self? Write about ways to embrace your unique timing without comparing yourself to others.

Setting Boundaries and Prioritising Self-Care:

Reflect on areas of your life where you may need to establish clearer boundaries to protect your energy and well-being. How can you show yourself kindness by prioritising self-care and setting limits on your time and energy commitments? Write about specific actions you can take to honour your own needs and create a nurturing environment that supports your Manifestor nature.

_____
_____
_____
_____
_____
_____
_____
_____
_____
_____
_____
_____
_____
_____
_____
_____
_____
_____
_____
_____
_____
_____
_____
_____
_____

Celebrating Your Initiations and Accomplishments

Take a moment to acknowledge and celebrate the manifestations and initiatives you have brought to life. Reflect on your past achievements, big or small, and recognize the courage and determination it took to bring them into reality. How can you show yourself kindness by celebrating your successes and giving yourself credit for the progress you've made? Write about ways to honour and appreciate your own accomplishments.

_____
_____
_____
_____
_____
_____
_____
_____
_____
_____
_____
_____
_____
_____
_____
_____
_____
_____
_____
_____
_____
_____

Practising Self-Compassion in Decision-Making

Reflect on times when you've made decisions that didn't go as planned or encountered resistance from others. How can you show yourself kindness by cultivating self-compassion in those moments? Write about ways to offer yourself understanding, forgiveness, and gentleness when things don't go according to your expectations. Explore self-soothing practices that can help you navigate any disappointment or frustration that may arise.

_____
_____
_____
_____
_____
_____
_____
_____
_____
_____
_____
_____
_____
_____
_____
_____
_____
_____
_____
_____
_____
_____

Cultivating a Supportive Inner Dialogue

Reflect on the language and thoughts you use when speaking to yourself. How can you show yourself kindness by cultivating a more supportive and empowering inner dialogue? Write about affirmations or positive statements that resonate with you as a Manifestor, and practise incorporating them into your daily self-talk. Explore ways to reframe self-criticism into self-compassion and kindness.

_____
_____
_____
_____
_____
_____
_____
_____
_____
_____
_____
_____
_____
_____
_____
_____
_____
_____
_____
_____
_____

A Letter to your Past Self

Writing a letter to your past self is an opportunity to reflect on your journey and offer guidance and support from your present perspective. Use these prompts as a starting point, but feel free to explore any other thoughts, insights, or experiences you would like to share with your past self. Approach the letter-writing process with kindness, compassion, and a genuine desire to offer support and encouragement to your past self.

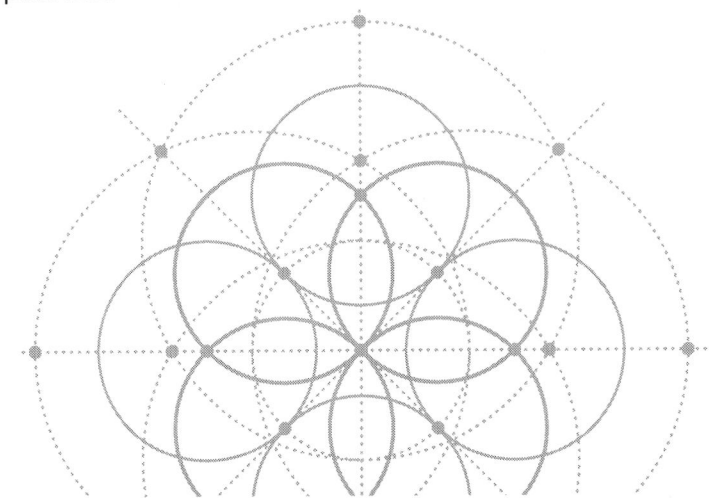

Embracing Your Manifestor Nature

Reflect on the journey of discovering your Manifestor nature. What advice or insights would you offer to your past self as they start to understand and navigate their unique energetic blueprint? Write about embracing your Manifestor power, honouring your autonomy, and trusting your instincts. Share any wisdom you've gained about initiating and manifesting from a place of authenticity.

_____
_____
_____
_____
_____
_____
_____
_____
_____
_____
_____
_____
_____
_____
_____
_____
_____
_____
_____
_____
_____
_____
_____

Trusting Your Inner Voice

Consider the times when you may have doubted your own inner voice or ignored your gut instincts. What would you like to say to your past self about the importance of trusting your intuition and inner knowing? Write about the significance of listening to your own guidance and the positive outcomes that can arise when you follow your authentic impulses.

_____
_____
_____
_____
_____
_____
_____
_____
_____
_____
_____
_____
_____
_____
_____
_____
_____
_____
_____
_____
_____
_____
_____
_____

Embracing Imperfections and Lessons

Reflect on the challenges, setbacks, or moments of self-doubt you've encountered along your journey as a Manifestor. What would you like to share with your past self about embracing imperfections and viewing them as valuable lessons? Write about the growth and resilience that can arise from facing difficulties and the importance of self-compassion in navigating those experiences.

Nurturing Self-Care and Boundaries

Consider the times when you may have neglected self-care or struggled with setting healthy boundaries. What advice would you give your past self about the importance of prioritising self-care and establishing boundaries that honour your energetic needs? Write about specific self-care practices and boundary-setting strategies that you've found beneficial as a Manifestor.

_____
_____
_____
_____
_____
_____
_____
_____
_____
_____
_____
_____
_____
_____
_____
_____
_____
_____
_____
_____
_____
_____
_____
_____
_____

Celebrating Your Manifestations

Reflect on the manifestations and initiatives you have successfully brought into reality as a Manifestor. What words of encouragement and celebration would you like to offer your past self? Write about the significance of acknowledging and celebrating your accomplishments, big or small, and the resilience and determination it took to manifest them.

_____
_____
_____
_____
_____
_____
_____
_____
_____
_____
_____
_____
_____
_____
_____
_____
_____
_____
_____
_____
_____
_____
_____
_____
_____

Writing to your Future Self

Writing a letter to your future self is a powerful exercise in envisioning and manifesting your desires. Use these prompts as a starting point, but feel free to delve into any other thoughts, aspirations, or visions you would like to share with your future self. Approach the letter-writing process with excitement, intention, and a genuine belief in your ability to manifest a fulfilling and purposeful future.

Embracing Your Manifestor Power

Imagine yourself in the future, fully embodying your Manifestor nature. What advice or affirmations would you offer to your future self about embracing your power and initiating with confidence? Write about the importance of trusting your instincts, honouring your autonomy, and manifesting from a place of authenticity. Encourage your future self to continue embracing your unique gifts and making a positive impact in the world.

_____
_____
_____
_____
_____
_____
_____
_____
_____
_____
_____
_____
_____
_____
_____
_____
_____
_____
_____
_____

Manifesting Bold Dreams and Visions

Envision the dreams, aspirations, and visions you have for your future self as a Manifestor. Write about the specific manifestations and initiatives you hope to bring into reality. Describe the steps you imagine taking to accomplish these goals and offer words of encouragement to your future self as you pursue your passions. Emphasise the importance of persevering, trusting your instincts, and staying true to your vision.

_____
_____
_____
_____
_____
_____
_____
_____
_____
_____
_____
_____
_____
_____
_____
_____
_____
_____
_____
_____
_____
_____
_____

Cultivating Boundaries and Self-Care

Consider the role of boundaries and self-care in your future as a Manifestor. Write about the strategies and practices you envision implementing to honour your energetic needs and protect your well-being. Encourage your future self to prioritise self-care, establish healthy boundaries, and communicate your needs with confidence. Remind yourself of the importance of balancing your autonomy with harmonious connections and relationships.

_____
_____
_____
_____
_____
_____
_____
_____
_____
_____
_____
_____
_____
_____
_____
_____
_____
_____
_____
_____
_____
_____
_____
_____
_____
_____

Embracing Adaptability and Growth

Reflect on the potential challenges, changes, and growth you anticipate in your future as a Manifestor. Write about the resilience and adaptability you envision cultivating as you navigate these experiences. Encourage your future self to view challenges as opportunities for growth, to embrace change with an open mind, and to trust in your ability to manifest positive outcomes even in uncertain times.

_____
_____
_____
_____
_____
_____
_____
_____
_____
_____
_____
_____
_____
_____
_____
_____
_____
_____
_____
_____
_____
_____
_____
_____

Celebrating Achievements and Milestones

Envision the future accomplishments, manifestations, and milestones you anticipate as a Manifestor. Write a letter filled with celebration and acknowledgment for the achievements you've reached and the goals you've realised. Express pride, joy, and gratitude for the progress you've made and encourage your future self to continue celebrating each step along your journey.

_____
_____
_____
_____
_____
_____
_____
_____
_____
_____
_____
_____
_____
_____
_____
_____
_____
_____
_____
_____
_____
_____
_____
_____
_____
_____
_____
_____

Difficult Situations

Writing about difficult situations can provide you with a sense of clarity, growth, and empowerment. Approach these prompts with a mindset of self-reflection and growth, allowing yourself to explore your experiences, emotions, and strengths as a Manifestor. Use writing as a tool for self-discovery, healing, and transformation.

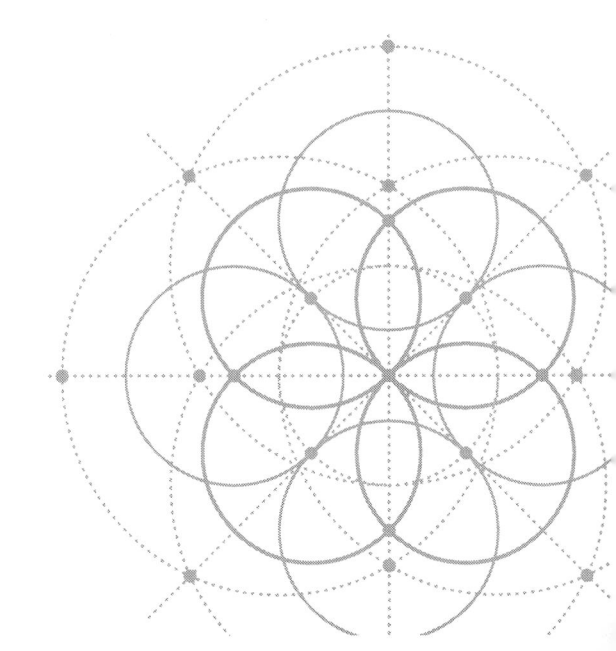

Reflecting on Lessons Learned

Think about a challenging situation you've faced as a Manifestor. What valuable lessons or insights did you gain from that experience? Write about the specific lessons you learned and how they have contributed to your growth and development. Explore how you can apply these lessons in future situations to navigate challenges with greater wisdom and resilience.

Expressing Emotions and Processing Feelings

Writing can be a powerful tool for emotional expression and processing. Take a moment to reflect on a difficult situation that evoked strong emotions within you. Write about the emotions you experienced and allow yourself to express them freely on paper. Explore how writing about these emotions can provide you with a sense of release, clarity, and understanding.

_____
_____
_____
_____
_____
_____
_____
_____
_____
_____
_____
_____
_____
_____
_____
_____
_____
_____
_____
_____
_____
_____
_____

Identifying Empowering Actions

Consider a difficult situation in which you felt a sense of disempowerment or resistance. Reflect on the actions you took or could have taken to regain a sense of empowerment and agency. Write about specific actions that align with your Manifestor nature and how you can apply them in similar situations to reclaim your power and initiate positive change.

_____
_____
_____
_____
_____
_____
_____
_____
_____
_____
_____
_____
_____
_____
_____
_____
_____
_____
_____
_____
_____
_____
_____

Setting Boundaries and Communicating Needs

Think about a challenging situation where boundaries were crossed or communication breakdowns occurred. Reflect on how you can show up more effectively as a Manifestor by setting clear boundaries and communicating your needs. Write about specific ways you can improve your communication skills, assertively express your boundaries, and navigate challenging conversations with grace and clarity.

Cultivating Self-Compassion and Resilience

Difficult situations can be emotionally draining and testing. Reflect on how you can show yourself kindness and compassion during challenging times. Write about ways to nurture your well-being, prioritise self-care, and cultivate resilience as a Manifestor. Explore self-soothing practices, supportive affirmations, and mindset shifts that can help you navigate difficult situations while maintaining inner balance and strength.

_____
_____
_____
_____
_____
_____
_____
_____
_____
_____
_____
_____
_____
_____
_____
_____
_____
_____
_____
_____
_____
_____
_____
_____
_____

You have chosen to spend this time with yourself, putting your needs first and devoting some time to self-discovery, self-understanding, and self-acceptance. By doing this work to strengthen yourself, you will find you have more to offer those around you, as you meet them from your solid foundation. Every investment in yourself is an investment in the world!

Thank You

Made in the USA
Columbia, SC
10 March 2025